THE WORLD ON THE MOVE
WATER TRAVEL

Eryl Davies

Thomson Learning

New York

THE WORLD ON THE MOVE
Air Travel

Rail Travel

Road Travel

Water Travel

All words that appear in **bold** are explained in the glossary.

First published in the
United States in 1993 by
Thomson Learning
115 Fifth Avenue
New York, NY 10003

First published in 1992 by
Wayland Publishers Ltd

Copyright © 1992 Wayland Publishers Ltd

U.S. version copyright © 1993 Thomson Learning

Library of Congress Cataloging-in-Publication Data
Davies, Eryl.
    Water travel / Eryl Davies.
      p.   cm. -- (The World on the move)
    Includes bibliographical references and index.
    Summary: Covers different trypes of vessels and their uses, the technology involved, and future developments in water travel.
    ISBN 1-56847-038-X : $14.95
    1. Ships--Juvenile literature. 2. Boats and boating--Juvenile literature. [1. Boats and boating. 2. Ships.] I. Title. II. Series.
VM150.D38 1993
387.2--dc20   93-7074

Printed in Italy

CONTENTS

Early ships	4
Sailing the high seas	6
Early steamships	8
Modern steamships	10
Work and vacation	12
Carrying cargo	14
The world's most important canals	16
Special purpose vessels	18
Docks and harbors	20
Safety and rescue technology	22
Modern technology for navigation	24
Water sports	26
The future	28
Glossary	30
Books to read	31
Index	32

Egyptian papyrus raft

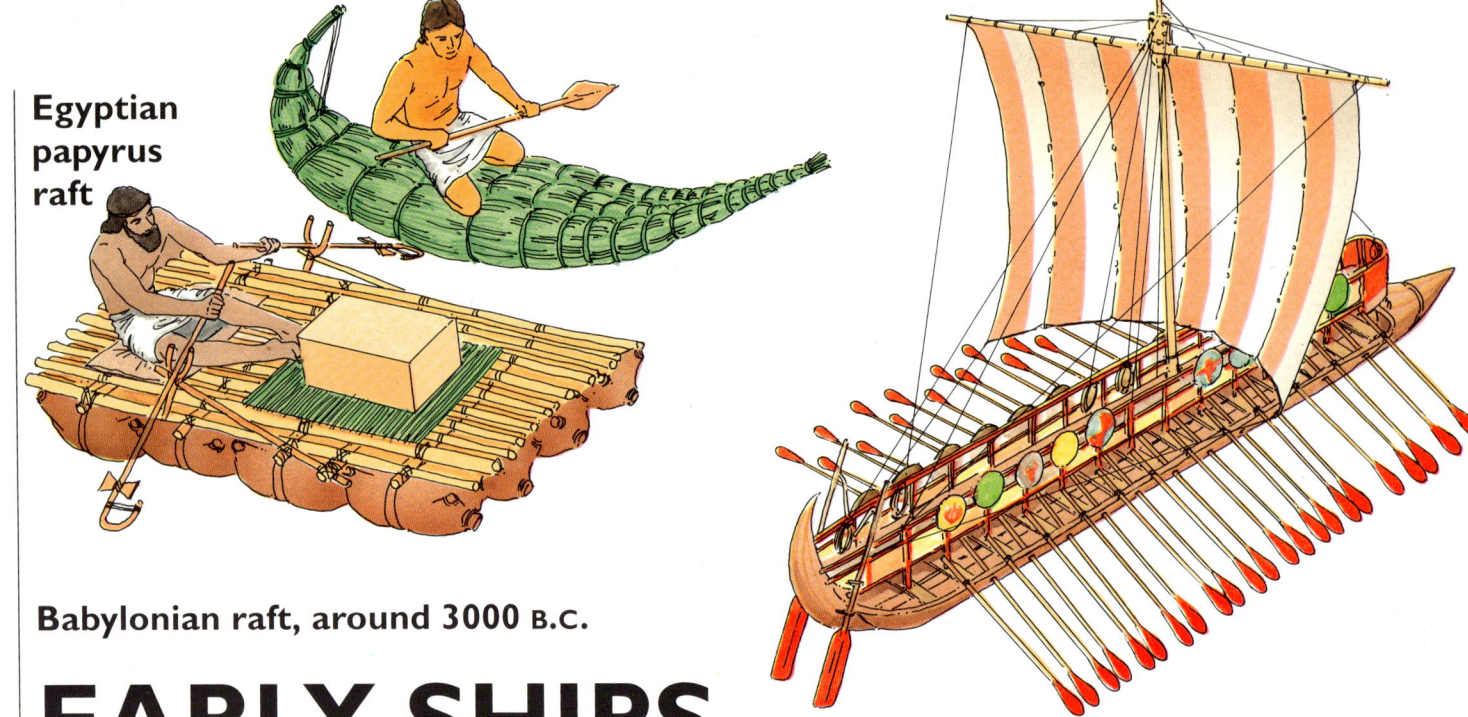

Babylonian raft, around 3000 B.C.

EARLY SHIPS

From the earliest times to the present, people have traveled by water to fish, trade, explore, conquer, or settle. In cities like Venice, Italy, and Bangkok, Thailand, water transportation is a necessary part of everyday life. People shop at floating markets and go to their jobs by boat.

Water transportation has taken many forms, from primitive canoes and rafts to modern steam-powered craft. The first

Phoenician *bireme* (war galley), 700 B.C.

boat builders were the ancient Egyptians and the **Sumerians**. About 5,000 years ago, they made vessels from wooden planks and bundles of reeds. The Egyptians added sails after 2900 B.C. to take them to nearby countries for trade. By 1500 B.C., Polynesians traveled the Pacific Ocean by raft and canoe. They settled in Melanesia and other island chains.

Viking longship, around A.D. 900

Roman merchant ship, A.D. 150

Greek trireme (war galley), 500 B.C.

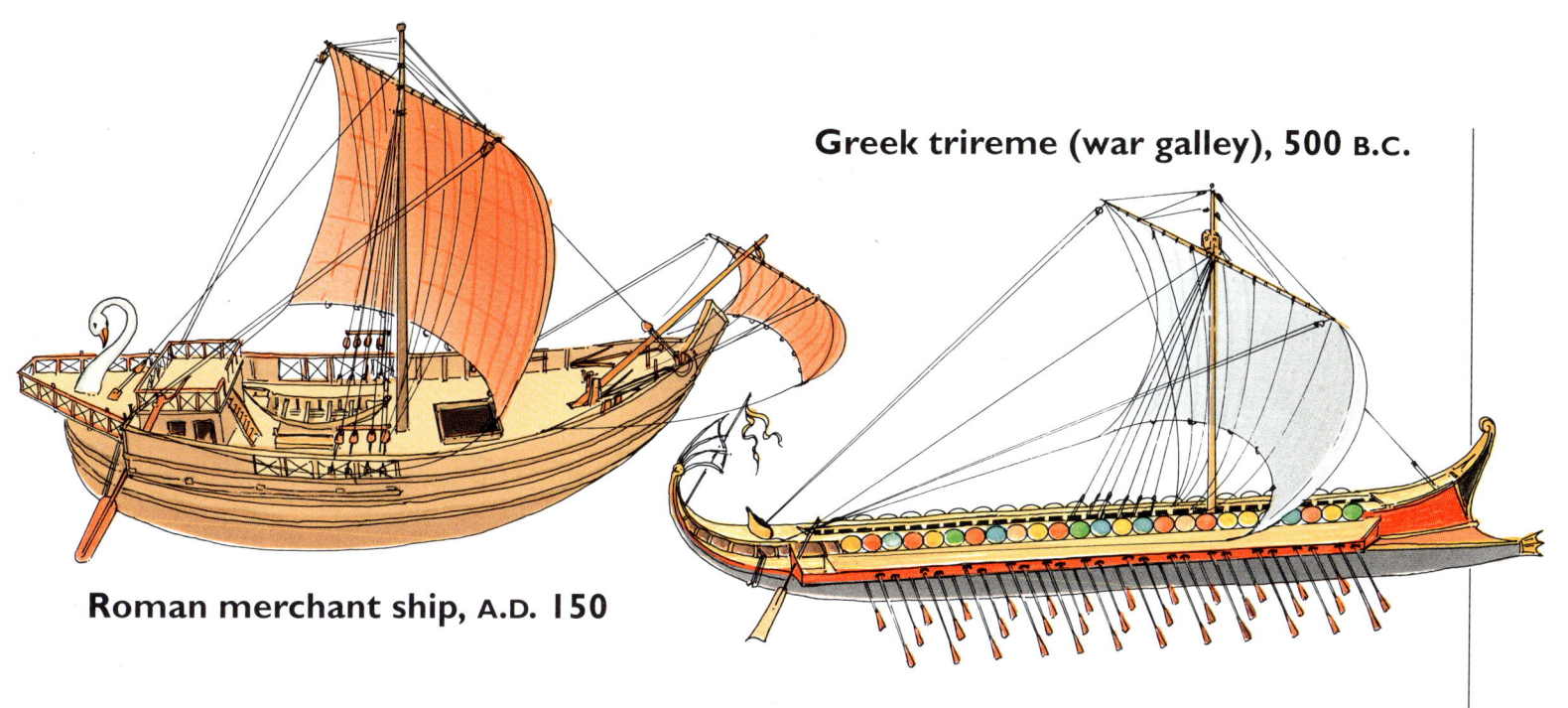

The **Phoenicians**, Greeks, and Romans fought naval battles with their war galleys around 500 B.C. From A.D. 800 until 1070, the Vikings used longships to conquer parts of Europe and explore the eastern tip of North America. They introduced the clinker method of making wooden **hulls**, using overlapping planks. Clinker-built ships were popular for a long time.

In the 1400s, trading ships and warships in northern Europe began to use carvel-built hulls, with planks fitted edge to edge over a frame. At this time, **superstructures**, such as the raised "castles" at the **bows** and **sterns** of larger warships, also appeared. Stern-mounted rudders replaced **quarter-rudders** for steering. At first, a large lever, rather than a wheel, was used to work the rudder, so ships needed gangs of men to steer them. Single sails were replaced by a number of sails supported on three masts. Sailors also learned that triangular **lateen** sails enabled them to sail even when the wind was not blowing in the direction they wanted to go.

Ship of the Cinque Ports, 1280

English ship, 1426

5

HIGH SEAS

The Europeans sailed the high seas as traders. They wanted to bring back precious spices from India without traveling the dangerous overland route. In their quest to find a fast and direct waterway to India, they ushered in the age of exploration.

In 1492, Christopher Columbus tried to reach India by sailing west, but landed in the West Indies instead. His flagship, the *Santa Maria*, a three-masted Spanish trading ship, was wrecked off the coast of Haiti. He took command of a smaller ship, the *Niña*, a Portuguese **caravel**, more suitable for exploration. On later voyages, he explored many Caribbean islands and the coast of Central America. Columbus opened the way for Europeans to settle in the Americas.

In 1620, the Pilgrims sailed to North America on an ordinary trading ship, the *Mayflower*. They were among the first European settlers on the continent. Others would soon follow them across the ocean.

A century later, the trading ships carrying cargo from Asia to Europe were bigger and faster. They had to carry guns to defend themselves from pirates. Between 1768 and 1779, the great English explorer Captain James Cook sailed the coal-carriers *Endeavour* and *Resolution* to discover Australia and New Zealand.

By the mid-1800s, the swiftest sailing ships were the **clippers**, used for trade with China. The most famous, the *Cutty Sark* of 1869, had a **tonnage** of 963. She was as fast as she was elegant and could exceed 15 **knots**, or 18 mph. Whether for trade, exploration, or settlement, sailing had been the most effective means of water travel. However, in the 1800s, sailing ships were being replaced by steamships, which were faster and capable of carrying more cargo.

DID YOU KNOW?
The largest sailing ship was the five-masted 6,390-ton *France II*, which was launched in 1911. The 5,730-ton United States ship *Thomas W Lawson*, built in 1902, had seven masts. The tallest was nearly 200 ft above deck.

The *Cutty Sark* at anchor in Falmouth harbor, Cornwall, England

Columbus's first flagship, *Santa Maria,* **was only 92 ft long.**

EARLY STEAMSHIPS

Early steamships were slow, cumbersome, and undependable. They were not ready to compete with sailing ships for cargo and passengers. In 1819, the *Savannah* became the first ship with a steam engine to cross the Atlantic. She departed from Georgia and reached Liverpool, England, in twenty-seven days. She had both sails and paddles because her crude engines, only used for three days during the crossing, needed too much fuel and were not reliable. When the *Savannah* was sighted off the coast of Ireland, she was mistakenly reported to be on fire!

By the late 1830s, steam engines had improved. In 1837, the 775-ton *Sirius* became the first ship to cross the North Atlantic using steam alone. In 1843, a British engineer named Isambard Kingdom Brunel launched the *Great Britain*, the first ocean-going ship built of iron. She was also one of the first large ships to have a propeller, although she also had paddles.

The first steam engines were only able to drive paddles. Inside the engine, steam power was used to make pistons move up and down. The pistons were connected to a shaft. The pistons' movement turned the shaft, which then made the paddles go around. Eventually it became possible to build engines without pistons, connected directly to propellers through the propeller shaft. This gradually caused the paddle-steamers to disappear.

The *Savannah*, showing the angled funnel that kept sparks away from the sails

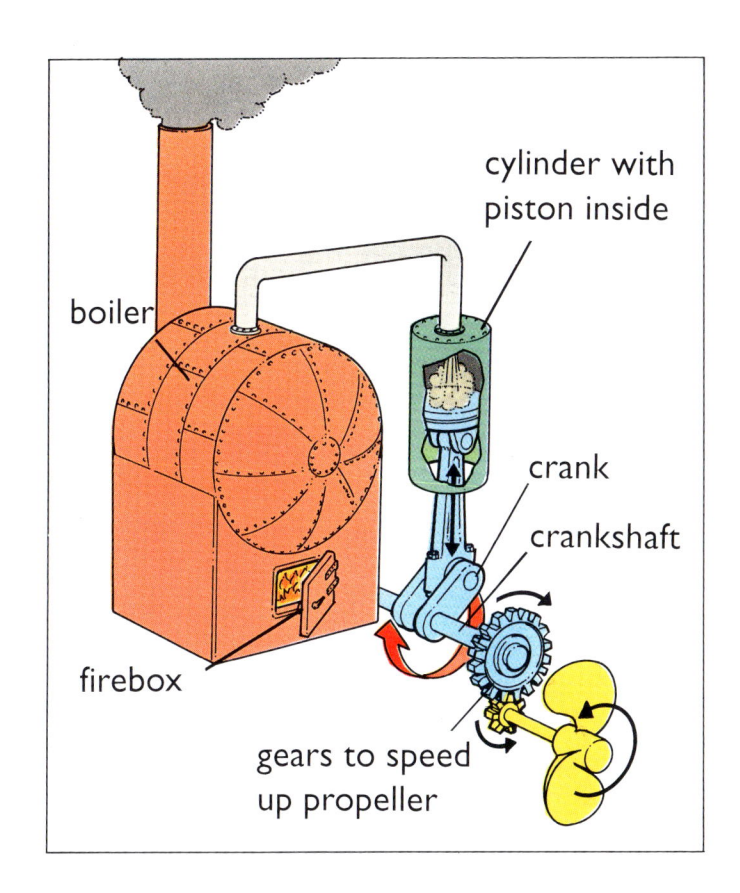

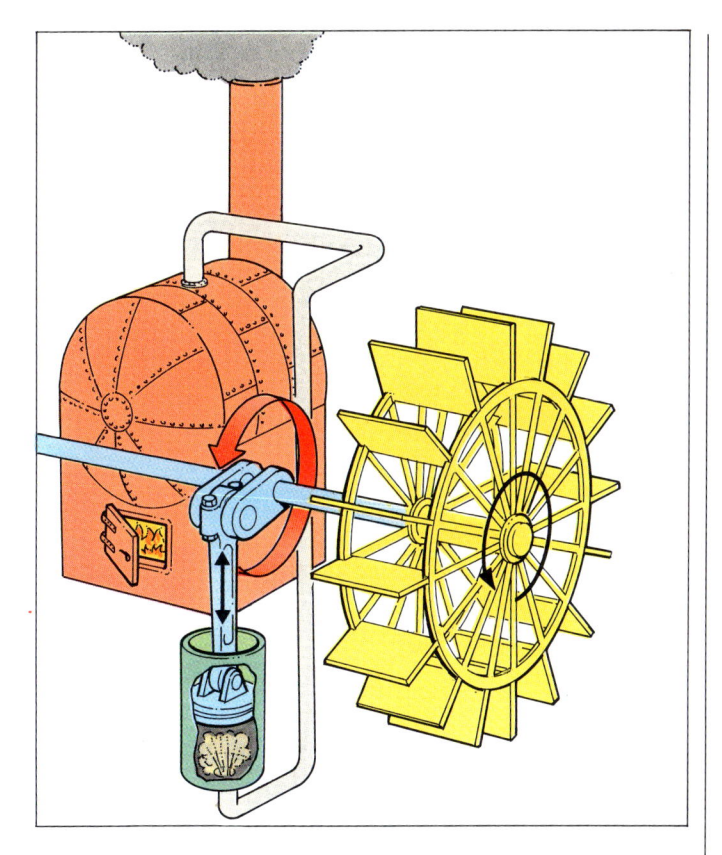

Early ways of connecting a steam engine to a propeller (left) and a paddle (right)

Even in the 1880s, new steamships were built with sails. The high price of coal, and engine breakdowns, still made sails essential. The *City of Paris* set new standards in 1889. She had twin engines and propellers, making breakdowns much less likely, and she needed only very small sails. Her hull was divided into fifteen separate compartments. When she ran aground off Cornwall in England, only one compartment flooded. She remained afloat and was repaired.

The *City of New York*

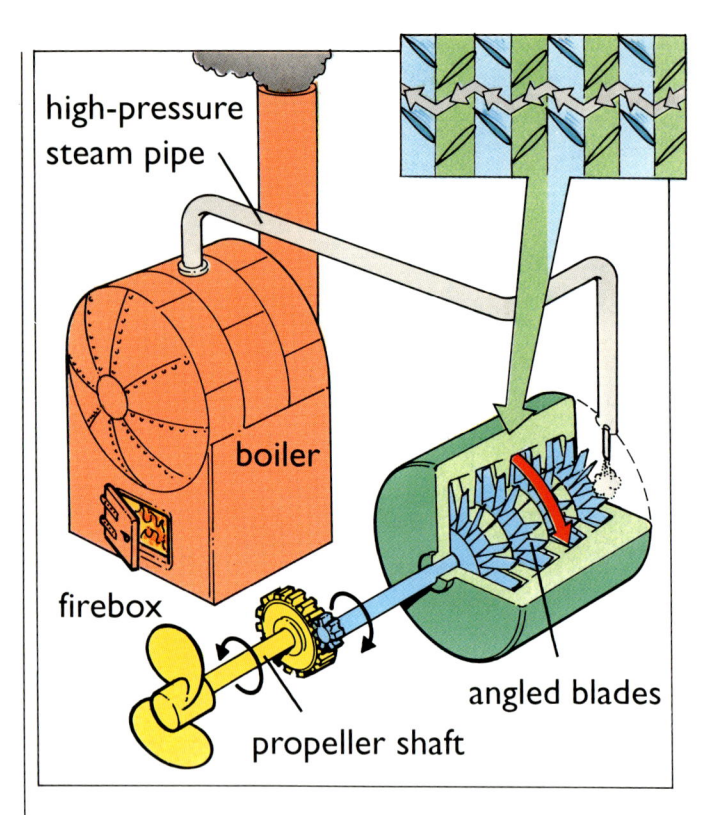

The steam turbine has fewer moving parts and can spin faster than other steam engines.

MODERN STEAMSHIPS

Steamship technology improved with the development of the turbine and diesel engines. Unlike the original steam engines, the turbine engine has rows of angled blades connected to a shaft. High-pressure steam jets make the blades rotate, spinning the shaft at high speed. The spinning shaft turns the propellers. The 34,000-ton *Mauretania* and *Lusitania*, built in 1907, were the first big passenger liners to use steam turbine engines. The ships transported vacationers, diplomats, and business people across the world's oceans. Their top speed was 28 mph. *Normandie* (1935), *Queen Mary* (1936), and *Queen Elizabeth* (1939), all about 88,000 tons, could reach speeds of around 38 mph.

The world's first steam turbine vessel, *Turbinia*

The luxurious dining room on the *Queen Mary* seated 815.

The liners burned huge amounts of costly fuel. Oil proved more efficient than coal, but was still very expensive.

During World War II, the ocean liners carried troops rather than passengers. After the war, ocean liners went into decline. Transatlantic jet airliners began passenger service in 1958 and could transport travelers much more quickly and economically. The fuel shortages of the 1970s made the ships too expensive to use at all.

Meanwhile, marine diesel engines (huge versions of those used in trucks and buses) were improving rapidly. In a diesel engine, a mixture of oil vapor and air enters the engine's cylinders. It is squashed by the pistons until it explodes, pushing the pistons back down. More of the air/fuel mixture enters the cylinders and the process is repeated. The pistons are connected to a shaft, as in a steam engine. As they go up and down, the shaft's rotation drives the propellers.

Diesel engines are much more efficient than steam engines. The passenger liner *Queen Elizabeth II* was built in 1969 with steam turbines, but was fitted with diesel engines in 1986 to save fuel.

> **DID YOU KNOW?**
> In 1952 the *United States* captured the **Blue Riband** at an astonishing average speed of 41 mph. Fast steamships had raced each other unofficially for this title for nearly 100 years.

WORK AND VACATION

Today, many people use water transportation to get to and from work, or to go on vacation. Car ferries take them short distances across rivers and channels, while cruise ships travel longer distances on the high seas for vacationing pleasure.

Most car ferries use the **ro-ro** layout. The cars go below deck, with passengers above. Bow and stern doors allow vehicles to be driven on and off without reversing. Driving on and off is so simple that the cars' owners do it themselves. This cuts

One of the most famous cruise ships, the *Queen Elizabeth II*

A Caribbean cruise ship

down delays and makes more profit for the ferries' owners.

Ro-ro ships have to be loaded and unloaded carefully. They have **ballast** tanks in which the water level can be adjusted quickly by powerful pumps. This balances the ship as the vehicles are being driven on and off. There are double doors at each end. The inner doors are watertight. On the **bridge**, monitor screens or lights tell the crew that the doors are shut properly.

In the United States, cruise ships are a popular way of transporting vacationers around the Caribbean, the coast of Alaska, and other locations. Most passengers fly to the ship's home port to board the vessel. Then they can enjoy more time at sea. The newest ships are like floating luxury hotels, similar to the huge Atlantic liners of the 1930s. However, they travel at slower speeds.

Some people prefer to take more unusual water transportation during their vacations. They travel as passengers on cargo ships to many parts of the world. Others cruise on icebreakers to participate in whale watches with expert guides.

Icebreakers have specially strengthened bows and hulls to stand up to the ice.

DID YOU KNOW?
The largest car and passenger ferry, the 64,330-ton *Silja Serenade*, operates between Stockholm in Sweden and Helsinki in Finland. The fastest, the 26,448-ton *Finnjet*, on the Finland-Germany route, can exceed 35 mph.

CARRYING CARGO

A tanker for carrying liquified natural gas from the Middle East

DID YOU KNOW?
One of the biggest ships ever built was the 622,342-ton tanker *Happy Giant*. She was 1,239 ft long and 225 ft wide. In 1980, she was lengthened to 266 ft when an extra section was added to her hull.

General mixed cargo, such as car parts, television sets, books, and furniture, is transported in containers. These are standard sized boxes, either 20 or 40 feet long. They fit on trucks and train cars, and they can be lifted directly onto a ship. Container ships have racks on top of each other to keep the cargo firmly in position during the journey. Special cranes are used to stack the containers, one above the other, in the racks.

Many ships are built for special cargoes. Some of the largest ships built have been oil tankers. Liquefied gas (for example, fuels like butane and methane) is also carried by tanker. The gases only remain liquid if they are kept very cold. These ships carry cooling machinery (like a huge refrigerator) and have well-insulated tanks to keep the liquid gas cold enough. Refrigerated ships are also used for carrying produce such as meat and bananas. When bananas are harvested,

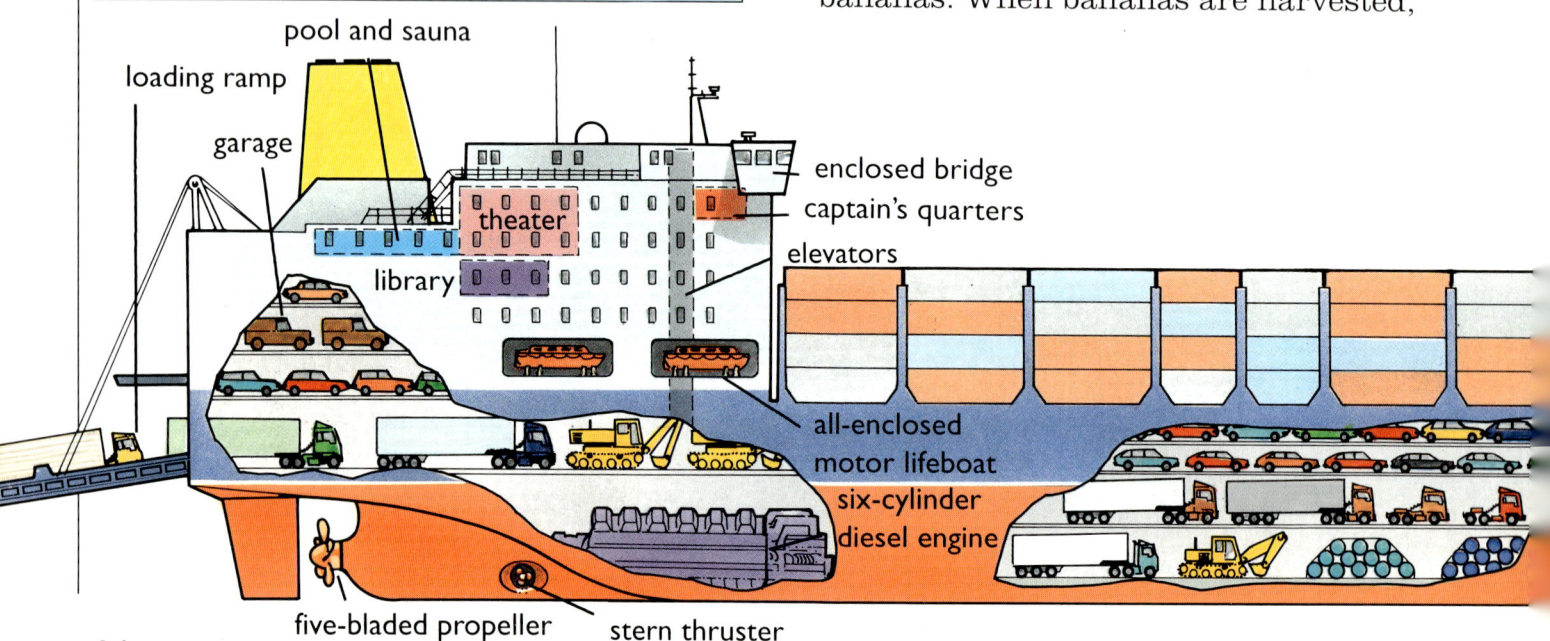

- pool and sauna
- loading ramp
- garage
- theater
- library
- enclosed bridge
- captain's quarters
- elevators
- all-enclosed motor lifeboat
- six-cylinder diesel engine
- five-bladed propeller
- stern thruster

A container ship at sea

This nine-cylinder diesel engine is about 58 ft long and 44 ft tall.

they are green. The temperature in the cargo hold is chosen so that when they arrive, they will have ripened.

Many large cargo ships are driven by a single engine and propeller. Some marine diesel engines produce more than 50,000 horsepower (hp), about 1,000 times more powerful than the engine of a car. Many container ships travel at about 25 mph. Their engines are very efficient, and they take up less space than steam turbine engines. They fit into a smaller engine room near the stern, leaving more room for cargo.

BELOW A 62,800-ton container vessel

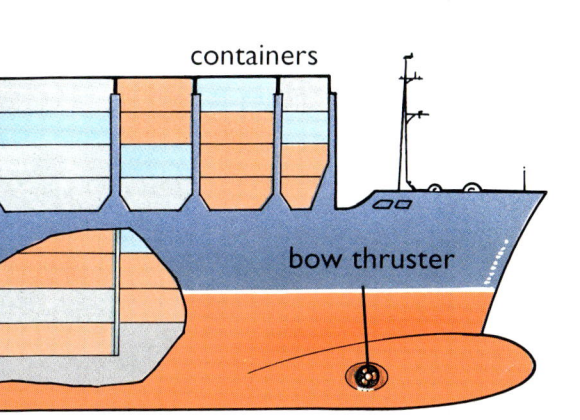

containers

car decks

bow thruster

general cargo

THE WORLD'S MOST IMPORTANT CANALS

The Suez Canal in Egypt links the Mediterranean Sea with the Red Sea. Opened in 1869, it is 100.6 miles long. It runs at sea level all the way, through the Bitter Lakes. The level of these changed when the canal was opened because of the small difference in levels between the Mediterranean and the Red Sea. It is now a vital route for ships traveling between Europe and the Far East.

The Panama Canal opened in 1914. It covers nearly 51 miles, linking the Pacific Ocean with the Caribbean. **Pilots** take control of ships from the time they enter the canal until they leave. The canal rises 85 feet above sea level, so ships have to go through six **locks**. These are very large—1,000 feet long and 110 feet wide. Going through the locks is such a delicate business that ships' engines cannot be used. They are drawn along by as many as eight electric locomotives, called "mules." These run on tracks beside the locks.

Ships cannot go at full speed through canals. Modern ships take about fifteen hours to pass through the Suez Canal. The Panama Canal is shorter and takes about eight hours. About half the time is spent in the locks—each one

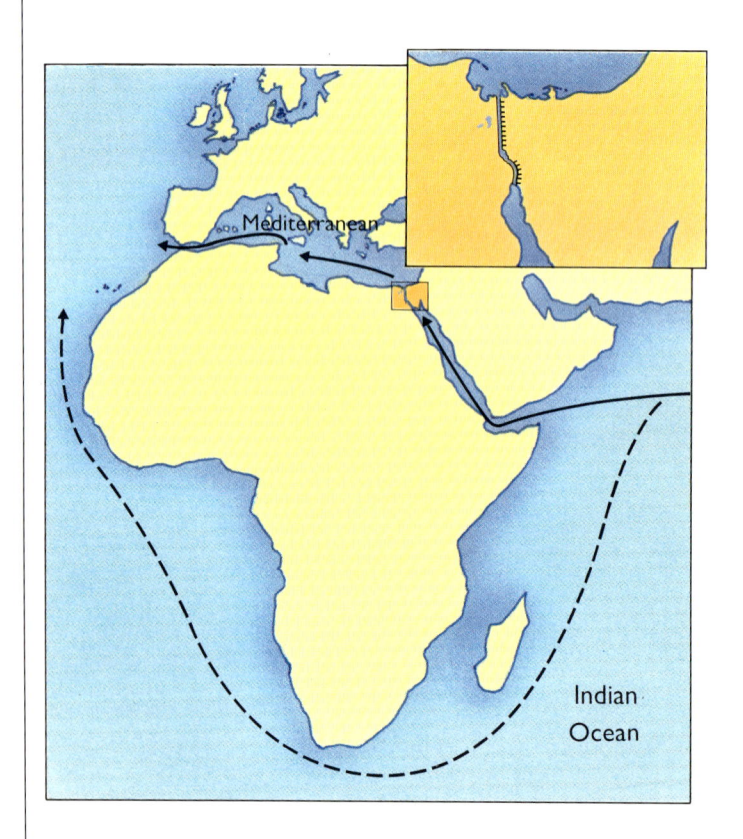

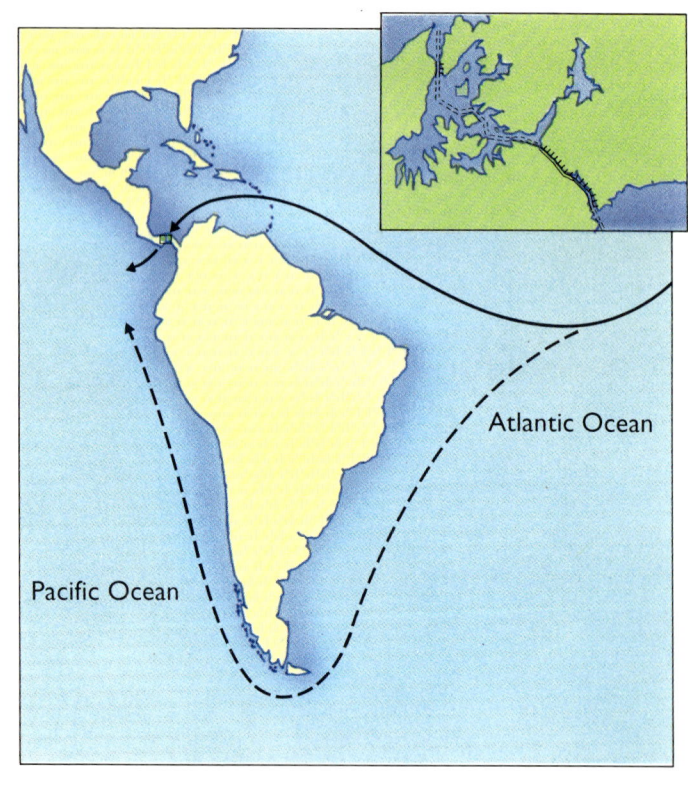

The Panama Canal (right) and Suez Canal (left) save ships thousands of miles in distance traveled.

A large container ship squeezing through one of the six locks on the Panama Canal

takes about an hour to get through. Even so, this is much quicker and safer than traveling thousands of miles around Cape Horn, the area of dangerous seas at the southern tip of South America.

DID YOU KNOW?
The biggest ship allowed through the Panama Canal is 108 ft wide—allowing just 1 ft on each side in the locks! The largest ship to pass through the Suez Canal was the 355,335-ton *Settebello*, which is 188 ft wide.

SPECIAL PURPOSE VESSELS

Some water transportation is for specific types of work. Fishing boats, surveying and drilling vessels, and cable ships are examples of special purpose crafts. Catching and transporting fish can be done by small boats as well as larger deep-water trawlers. Some use nets to catch fish swimming near the surface, and others scoop up fish from the seabed. Factory ships process and freeze the catch on board. Stern trawlers have tall frames above the stern, which lower a net into the sea, then haul the catch back on board. This leaves the forward part of the ship clear for sorting and packing the fish. All larger fishing vessels have depth-measuring and fish-detecting equipment to help the skipper locate schools of fish.

Drilling vessels search the seabed for new sources of oil and gas. Measurements taken from the surface can tell scientists where they are most likely to find oil and gas. Drilling vessels hover above a particular spot on the seabed, then make

The *Patria*, a high-speed SWATH ferry operating between Madeira and Porto Santo in the North Atlantic

DID YOU KNOW?
Although many countries would like to see it outlawed, whale killing still goes on; the largest whaling factory-ship is the 35,264-ton Russian vessel *Sovietska Ukrania*.

Sea Dog, a remote-control tracked vehicle that digs trenches for undersea cables

a test by drilling into the rocks below. Before oil production starts, special barges lay underwater pipelines from the wells to the shore. Divers are often needed to repair undersea pipelines. They work from diving support ships, which carry complex equipment and diving bells.

Cable ships install and repair undersea lines that carry telephone calls and data between continents. The North Atlantic has a network of cables that carry tens of thousands of telephone calls. Cable ships store thousands of miles of cable below deck. They may also carry remote-control vehicles called **submersibles** for inspecting cables or burying them under the seabed. Submersibles have also been used to locate and report on the condition of sunken ships believed to contain treasure or to have historical importance, such as the *Titanic*.

DOCKS AND HARBORS

If the approach to a port is tricky, a pilot will go on board to take over from the captain. He or she will have detailed knowledge of the local tides and narrow channels along the way into the harbor.

Modern ships have **side thrusters**. These allow the ship to be swung around in a small space, and to be gently moved sideways while docking. Even so, tugs are still needed to assist the bigger ships. They are often known as "water tractors." Most have diesel engines, ranging from a few hundred horsepower for harbor work to 25,000 horsepower for oceangoing tugs. Many have their propellers or **thrusters** fitted in the middle part of the ship. They are steered by swiveling the entire thruster, making the tug very agile. The thrusters are controlled by a simple control stick.

ABOVE **A ship being repaired in a dry dock at St. Malo, France**
BELOW **The *Queen Elizabeth II* being assisted by tugs in England's Southampton harbor**

In many harbors, channels deep enough for larger ships to pass through have to be kept clear. The constant movement of the water, due to tides and currents, often causes these channels to clog up with gravel, sand, or mud. Special vessels called dredgers are used to take care of this. They lift solid material from the bottom and take it away to be dumped.

Many larger harbors have dry dock facilities where ships can be taken out of the water for repairs. Normal dry docks have gates like lock gates. The ship goes into the dock, the gates are closed, and the water is pumped out. Floating docks work in a different way. The ship enters, and the floating dock's ballast tanks are pumped until empty. This lifts the dock and the ship inside it out of the water.

DID YOU KNOW?
The largest suction dredger is the *Prins der Nederlanden*, built in 1968. She can suck up 22,000 tons of sand in less than an hour through huge pipes, making a channel deep enough for a supertanker.

A special dredger keeping the approaches to the Panama Canal clear

SAFETY AND RESCUE TECHNOLOGY

Space satellites now play a vital role in making sea travel safer. The Global Maritime Distress and Safety System (GMDSS) is designed to give victims of disasters at sea the best possible chance of survival. All ships going beyond the reach of coastal radio stations will have Emergency Position-Indicating Radio Beacons (EPIRB) that send distress signals automatically if the ship is in trouble.

Satellites that continuously move around the earth keep constant watch. When they pick up a distress signal from an EPIRB, they relay details of the ship and her position to coastal stations. This allows the rescue to be coordinated on shore, and for help to be sent to the scene. Ships at sea are told that there is an emergency by radio messages from the coastal stations. They may also receive the news on Navsat — an information service especially for ships.

If the ship is in serious danger, the ship's lifeboats will then have to be launched. Modern ships' lifeboats can be launched more safely and quickly than those on old ships. Inflatable slide chutes (as used on aircraft) can be used to speed up

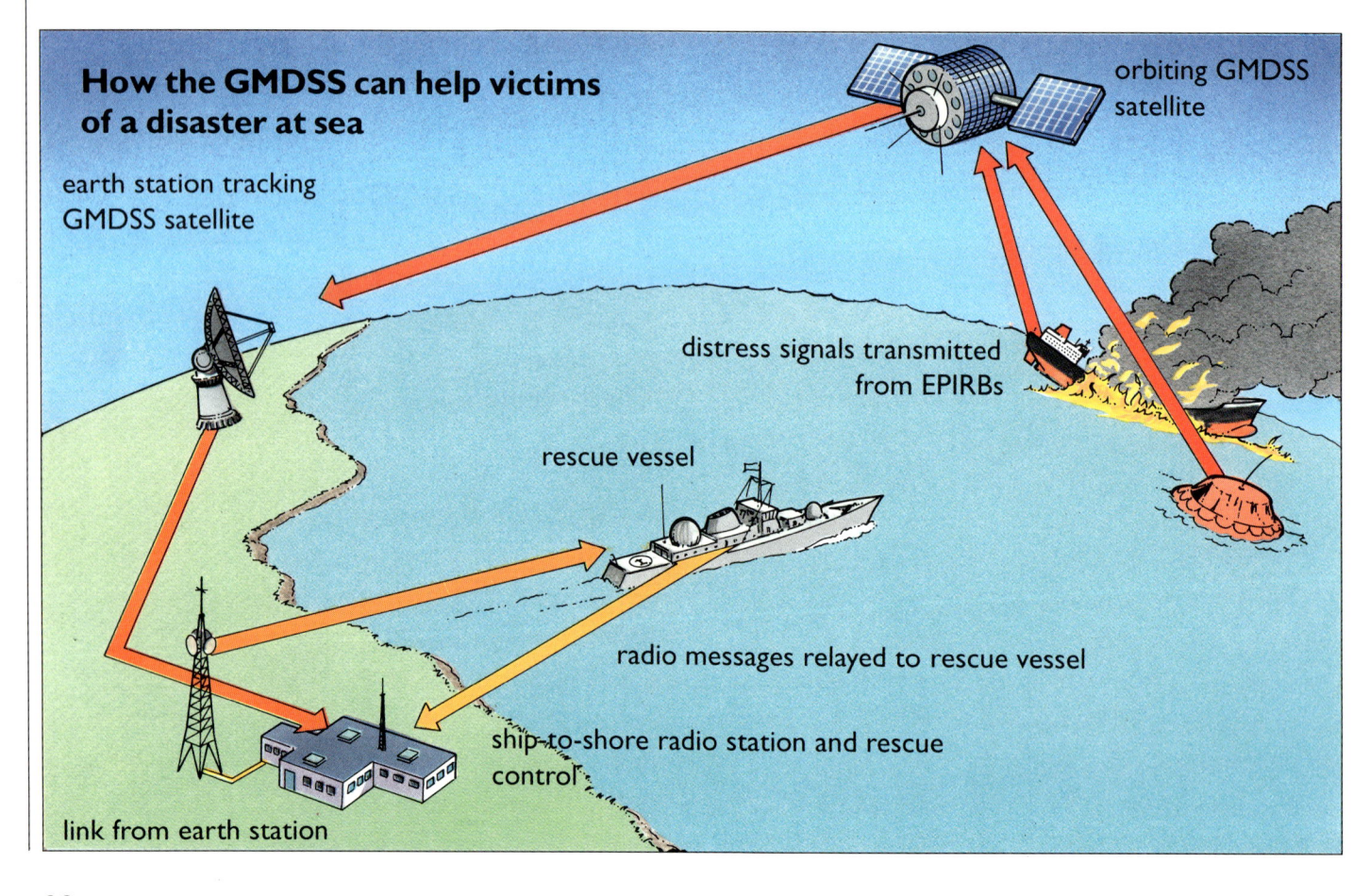

How the GMDSS can help victims of a disaster at sea

- orbiting GMDSS satellite
- earth station tracking GMDSS satellite
- distress signals transmitted from EPIRBs
- rescue vessel
- radio messages relayed to rescue vessel
- ship-to-shore radio station and rescue control
- link from earth station

The Coast Guard in action

evacuation. Ships sailing in places with severe weather conditions, or vessels in which fire is a major hazard (oil tankers, for example) have fully sealed capsules. The crew seal themselves in, and the capsule is launched down a chute. Some capsules can withstand temperatures of 2,000°F.

Radar can help people in lifeboats. Search and rescue **transponders** (SART) on board lifeboats pick up radar signals from ships searching for survivors. The SART replies with a special signal that appears as a dotted line on the radar screen of the rescue ship. To reassure survivors that someone is coming to rescue them, the SART makes bleeping sounds whenever it detects a ship's radar.

DID YOU KNOW?
Some disasters threaten our environment, rather than human life. In 1989, the 10-million-gallon oil spill from the tanker *Exxon Valdez* killed thousands of sea birds and other marine life off the coast of Alaska.

MODERN TECHNOLOGY FOR NAVIGATION

All the information about a ship's machinery, position, and progress can now be stored in computers and displayed on monitor screens. Very soon, ships will be controlled from a "workstation" on the bridge. The bridge will look more like an office, with computer screens and keyboards.

Color radar display screens in the control room at England's Southampton docks. Compare the map of the docks with the radar pictures.

All large ships now communicate via satellites. The **Inmarsat** organization has several satellites, hovering over the **equator**. These send radio signals between ships and land-based radio stations, which are linked to telephone networks. Machinery keeps the ship's antenna pointed at the satellite even if the ship is moving about in rough seas. The weatherproof plastic dome housing the antenna can be seen high on the superstructure. The ship's radio

24

equipment is so simple to use that radio operators are no longer necessary. The twenty-four-hour service via satellite is reliable, and means communication by radio between ship and shore is as clear as a local telephone call. Many kinds of messages go through these satellite links: instructions from the ship's owners, weather reports, information about navigation, and calls to home from the crew and passengers.

Satellites are also used for navigating. The Global Positioning System (GPS) has more than twenty satellites traveling around the earth every twelve hours. A special receiver on board ships picks up signals from the satellites and then works out the ship's position. Owners of small boats can buy hand-held GPS navigators. The system can tell the user the position of his or her ship to within a few feet anywhere in the world.

Radar allows the crew to "see" other ships, obstructions, and coastlines at night and in the fog. A ship's radar transmitter sends out powerful pulses of radio energy. Solid objects reflect some of the energy, and these "echoes" are picked up by the radio receiver. The receiver turns the echoes into pictures on a screen. Modern radar displays look like color computer displays.

A trawler's bridge. The radar scanners are just above the funnel.

A windsurfer showing off his skill near the coast of Venezuela

WATER SPORTS

Many people use water transportation as a form of recreation. Some take boats and yachts to go waterskiing or scuba diving. Others try pushing their skills to the limit by competing in sailing and yachting races.

Modern materials have transformed sporting and leisure craft. Plastics, especially fiberglass, have made modern boats and yachts easier to build and maintain. Designers can dream up smooth, curved shapes for fiberglass hulls. These hulls are also very strong without being heavy and are simple to repair.

Offshore power boats like this cigarette boat use large, highly tuned racing engines.

Ocean-going racing yachts like this can cost millions of dollars. They carry crews of about ten people. Each person has a special task to do, and they take turns on watch.

Fiberglass boats are made by brushing a layer of sticky resin into a hollow mold, and then laying a mesh of glass fibers on top. More resin is put on, and the process is repeated. When the resin hardens and the mold is taken away, a thin, tough shell remains. Even greater strength can be achieved (at a cost) if space-age materials like carbon fiber are used. The ultimate high-performance craft, which use such materials, include the tiny Formula 1 **hydroplanes**, the larger offshore power boat racers, and the enormously expensive yachts that compete in ocean racing. These use expensive metals in the **rigging** as well. Carbon fiber masts are common, and some are made of **titanium**.

All boats built especially for speed demand a lot from their crews. The 375 hp Formula 1 machine has neck-breaking acceleration and cornering. Offshore racers give their crews a pounding as they leap along crests of waves in the open sea. Ocean yacht crews endure cramped quarters, constant movement of the boat, and hard work in the worst conditions the oceans can offer.

Small solar-powered boat

SWATH passenger ship

THE FUTURE

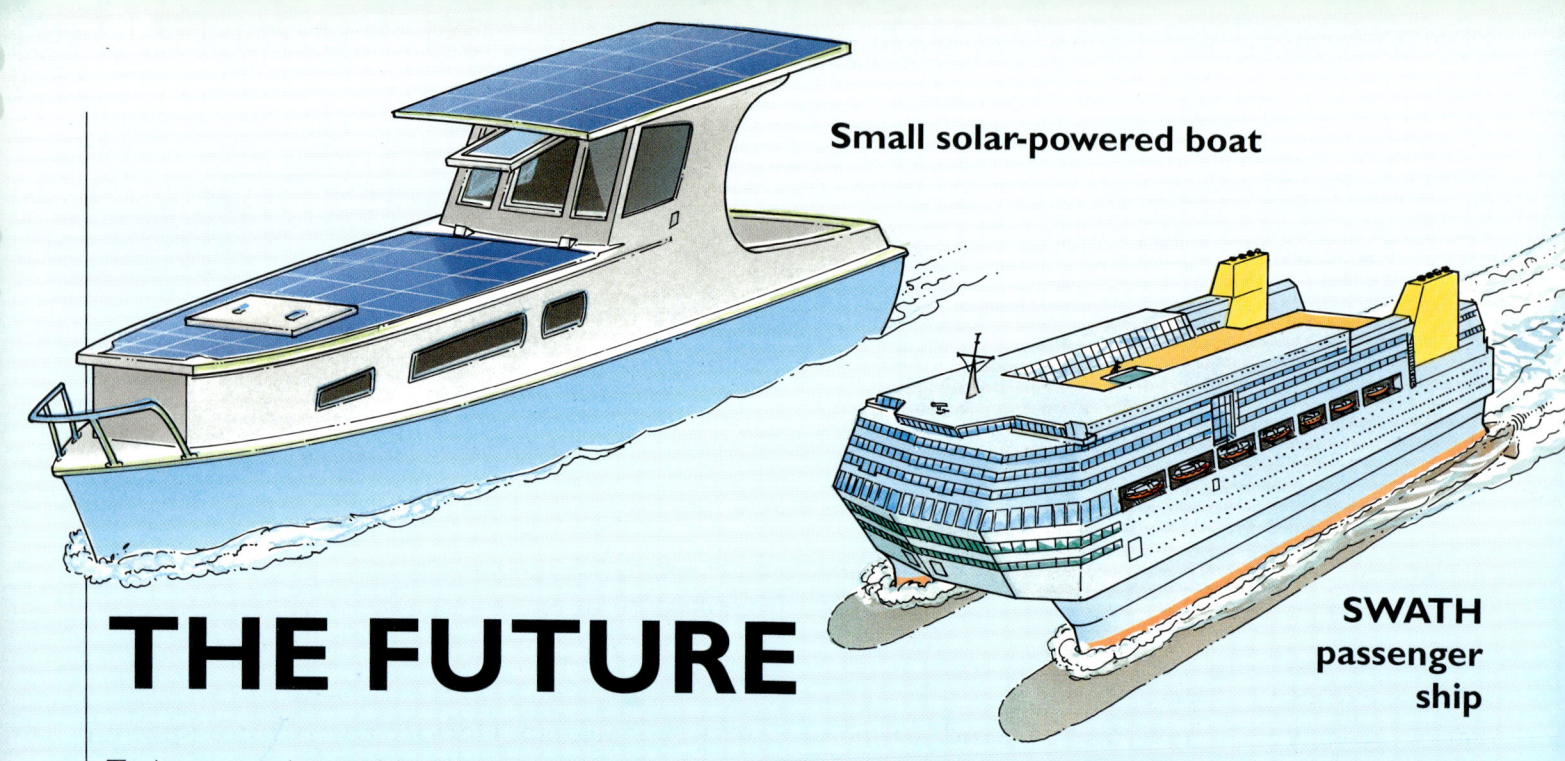

To transport people and cargo by water requires energy. Today there is concern that the oil and gas needed to power ships, as well as air, rail, and highway vehicles, may damage the planet. Also, supplies of these fossil fuels will one day be used up. That is why scientists are searching for alternative sources of energy.

For their size, ships are very low energy-users. For any heavy cargo that does not have to be moved quickly, ships are still the best means of transportation.

In the next few years, we can expect ships to become even more efficient. Changes to ships' hulls will allow them to slip through the water more easily and to use less fuel. Diesel engines and propellers will be improved. Propellers may even disappear completely. An experimental Japanese boat was tested in 1992. It uses electricity to produce a powerful jet of water that pushes the boat along.

Sail-assisted cargo vessel

Yamato I electric water-jet vessel

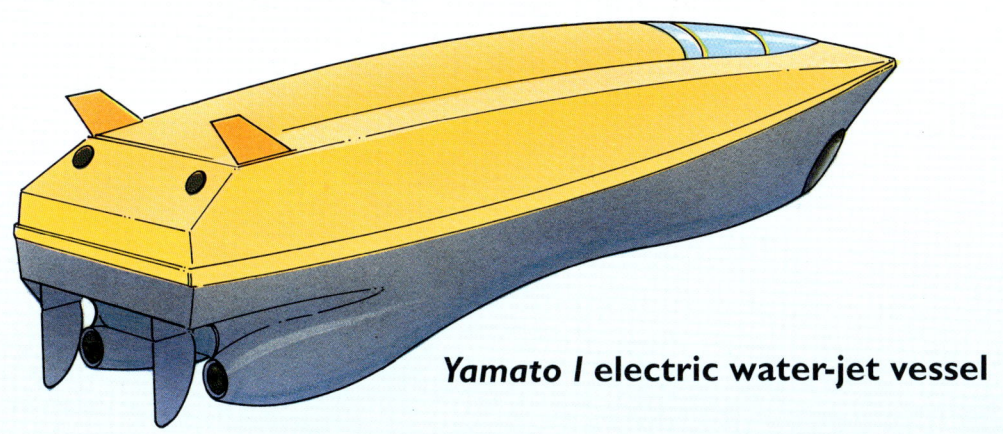

Ships of the future may be powered by forms of energy that will never run out, such as wind, solar (power from the sun), and nuclear power. There have already been successful trials of vessels that run on electricity produced by the wind. Like the old sailing ships, the problem of being stranded in calm weather remains. Back-up engines will still be needed until some way of storing the electricity is found. With solar power, however, there are solar batteries to store the power. Otherwise, a solar-powered vessel would come to a halt at night. Atomic power is a distant possibility. This has already been used to power nuclear submarines. However, fears about the safety of atomic power make using this form of energy questionable.

At present, aircraft carry many more passengers than ships. However, scientists have recently found that high-flying jet aircraft cause more damage to the atmosphere than other forms of transportation. Large high-speed passenger vessels, based on current twin-hull, or **SWATH**, designs are being developed. These may be able to compete with aircraft in terms of speed, and will cause less environmental damage.

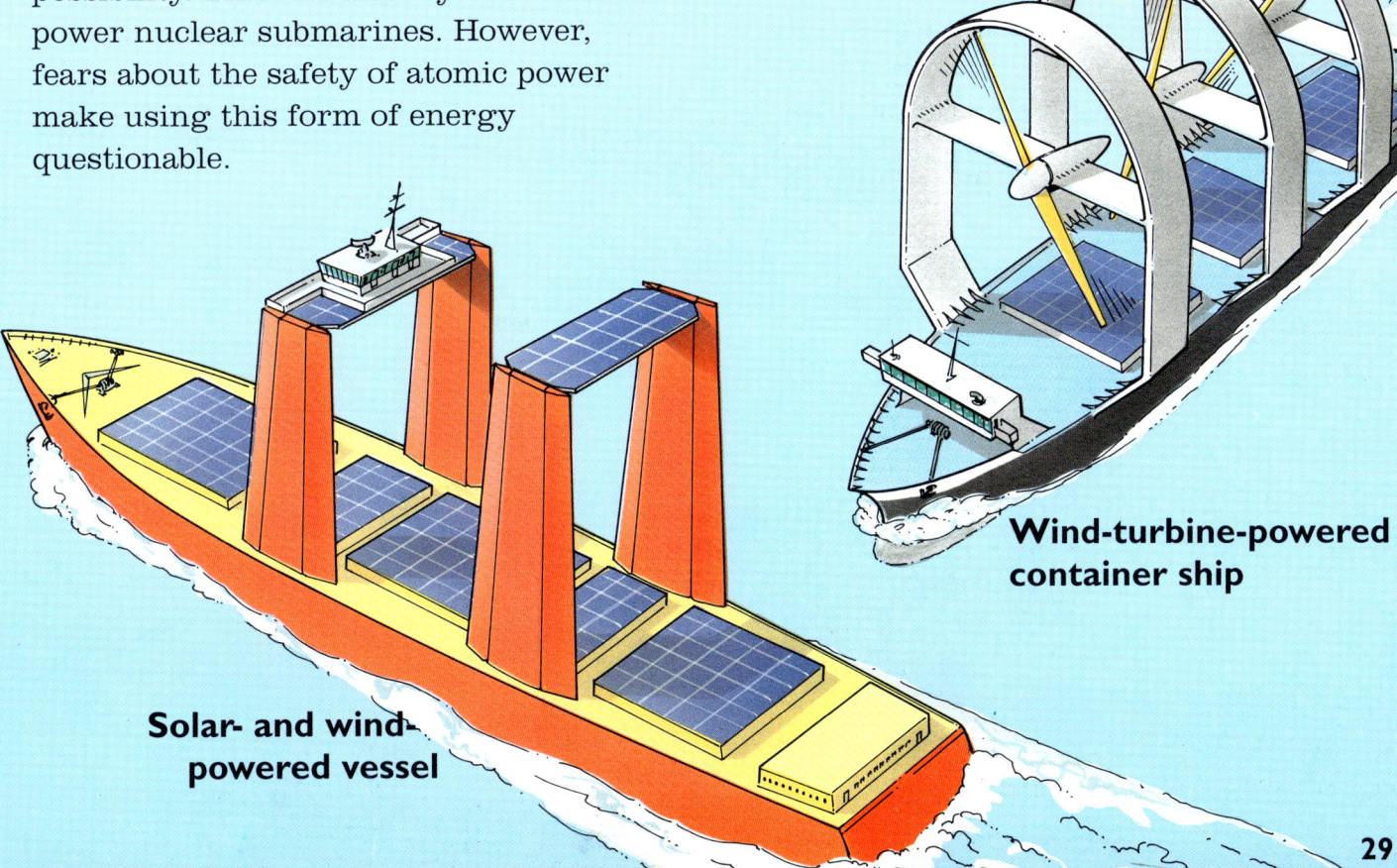

Solar- and wind-powered vessel

Wind-turbine-powered container ship

GLOSSARY

Ballast Heavy material (often water in modern ships) placed in the bottom of a ship. Without it, the ship would be top heavy and might capsize.
Blue Riband The record for the fastest journey across the Atlantic by a passenger ship.
Bow The front end of a ship.
Bridge The area of a ship from which it is commanded and navigated.
Caravel A small, light, and speedy ship. Caravels were usually Portuguese or Spanish and were common from the fifteenth to the seventeenth centuries.
Clipper A fast sailing ship with a swept-forward bow and swept-back masts.
Equator An imaginary circle around the middle of the earth halfway between the North and South poles.
Hull The main floating structure of a ship.
Hydroplane A high-speed motorboat that travels with its hull raised out of the water.
Inmarsat The International Maritime Satellite Organization, which provides satellites for communication at sea.
Knot A unit of speed at sea. One knot equals about 1.15 mph.
Lateen A triangular sail suspended from an arm mounted at 45° to the mast.
Lock A closed-off part of a canal where the water level changes. Vessels enter, watertight gates at each end are closed, and the water level can be raised or lowered.
Phoenicians The people of Phoenicia, an ancient country that is now part of the Middle East.

Pilot A person who is trained to steer ships in canals or harbors.
Quarter-rudder An old-fashioned rudder, almost like the oar of a rowboat, held over the side of a ship.
Rigging The ropes and cables of a ship.
Ro-ro Short for "roll-on/roll-off." A car ferry with doors at both ends.
Side thruster A thruster set so that it moves a ship sideways. It is usually mounted at the bow.
Stern The rear part of a ship.
Submersible A miniature submarine, with a crew of two or three, used for underwater surveys and repairs.
Sumerians The people of Sumeria, an ancient country that is now part of modern Iraq.
Superstructure Any part of a ship above the hull.
SWATH Stands for "Small Water-Area Twin Hull." An advanced ship design in which the accommodation cabins are supported on two slender tubes below water level.
Thruster A special type of propeller mounted in a tube.
Titanium A very light but strong metal. It is used to make many parts of the Concorde aircraft.
Tonnage A confusing description of a ship's size, and of what she can carry. Since it is impossible to weigh a ship, engineers calculate the tonnage by measuring the amount of space inside, and converting their results into tons.
Transponder A special radio or radar transmitter, usually mounted on a buoy. It only works when it receives signals from a ship.

BOOKS TO READ

Coote, Roger. *The Sailor Through History.* Journey Through History. New York: Thomson Learning, 1993.

Hamilton-MacLaren, Alistair. *Water Transportation.* Technology Projects. New York: Bookwright, 1992.

Humble, Richard. *Ships: Sailors and the Sea.* Timelines. New York: Franklin Watts, 1991.

Lambert, Mark. *Ship Technology.* Technology in Action. New York: Bookwright, 1990.

Ships and Boats. Let's Discover. Austin: Raintree Steck-Vaughn, 1983.

Spangenburg, Ray and Diane Moser *The Story of America's Canals.* New York: Facts on File, 1992.

Tunis, Edwin. *Oars, Sails and Steam: A Picture Book of Ships.* New York: HarperCollins, 1977.

Picture acknowledgments

The publishers would like to thank the following for the pictures used in this book: BT Marine 19, Mary Evans Picture Library 6, 8, 9, 10, 11; Eye Ubiquitous *cover*, 21, 25, 26 (top); FBM Marine Group 18; New Sulzer Deal Ltd. 15 (bottom); P & O Bulk 15 (top); William Payne/MBM 24; Quadrant Picture Library 26 (bottom), 27; Red Funnel Group 20 (bottom); Topham Picture Library 17, 20 (top), 23; Wayland Picture Library 12; Zefa Picture Library 13 (bottom).

The artwork is provided by Nick Hawken.

INDEX

Africa 6
Atlantic Ocean 8, 13, 18, 19
Australia 6, 8

bows 5, 13
Brunel, Isambard
    Kingdom 8

cable ships 19
canoes 4
Cape Horn 17
car ferries 12
cargo ships 14-15, 28
Caribbean, the 6, 13
clippers 6
Columbus, Christopher 6, 7
Cook, Captain 6
cruise ships 12-13
Cutty Sark, the 6

divers 19
docks 20-21, 24
dredgers 21
drilling vessels 18, 19

Egypt 4
electric locomotives 16
Emergency Position -
    Indicating Radio Beacons
    (EPIRB) 22
energy 28, 29
engines
    diesel 11, 15, 20, 28
    steam 8, 9, 10
    steam turbine 10, 15

England 5, 8-9
environment 23, 29
Europe 4, 6, 12, 16
Exxon Valdez 23

fiberglass 26, 27

Global Maritime Distress
    and Safety System
    (GMDSS) 22
Global Positioning System
    (GPS) 25

hulls 5, 13, 26

India 6

Japan 28

lifeboats 22, 23
locks 16

Mayflower, the 6
Mediterranean Sea 4, 16

Navsat 22
New Zealand 6

oil tankers 14, 23

Pacific Ocean 6, 16
Panama Canal 16-17, 21
pirates 6
propellers 8, 9, 28

Queen Mary, the 10, 11
Queen Elizabeth, the 10
Queen Elizabeth II, the
    11, 12, 20

racing ships 26-27
radar 23, 24, 25
radio 24-25
rafts 4
Red Sea 16
refrigerated ships 14
ro-ro ships 12
rudders 5

sails 4, 5, 6-7, 8-9
Santa Maria, the 6, 7
satellites 22, 23, 24, 25
scientists 19, 29
search and rescue
    transponders (SART) 23
steamships 6, 8-9
submersibles 19
Suez Canal 6, 16-17
superstructures 5

trading 6
trawlers 18
tugs 26

underwater pipelines 19

Vikings 4

32

10873

LOCUST GROVE ELEM. LIBRARY

DATE DUE

APR 12	APR 2 0 1996				
APR 19					
MAY 3					
FEB 2 0 1996					
FEB 1 0 1996					
FEB					
MAR 2 2 1996					

HIGHSMITH   # 45228